hung, **drawn** and quartered: THE CARICATURES OF KEN GILL

Hung, drawn and quartered – the caricatures of Ken Gill

Edited by John Green and Michal Boñcza

First published in Britain in 2009 by Artery Publications, 11 Dorset Road, London W5 4HU

Copyright © Artery Publications 2009

Photographs courtesy of Ken Gill private archive pp 3, 7, 8, 9, 10 11, 16, 28, 32, 44, 46, 56, 76, 84, 98, 92, 94, 100, 106; Andrew Wiard pp 54, 60, 66, 70, 80, 102, 110, 112 (Blair); Monire Childs pp 26, 50, 112 (Thatcher); Aslef pp 24, 78; Stefano Cagnoni p 52; TUC Library Collections London Metropolitan University p 30; Marx Memorial Library pp 32, 42; Re-elect Simpson Campaign p 98; Britannia Building Society p 82. Many of the other photos come courtesy of family archives. Some remain unattributed despite efforts made to identify the authors. We offer a sincere apology to those who might have been omitted as a result.

Caricatures by Ken Gill, Copyright©Ken Gill 2009

Designed by Michal Boñcza, www.artloud.com

Printed by Lithosphere Ltd (020 7868 6111)

ACIP catalogue record for this book is available from the British Library

ISBN 978-0-9558228-2-7

DEDICATION Firstly to my wife Norma, affectionate and forgiving, without whom nothing gets done properly. My children, Joe, Tom and Emma who are a constant source of love, criticism and pride to me. I have also been fortunate in my two stepdaughters Anita and Bridget.

The caricatures included here cover only a small proportion of those made over the years. I make no claims for them of artistic merit, but they are all done from life and the captions are my own.

I only regret that I could not find the one I drew of Arthur Nye, the shoemaker who opened my schoolboy eyes on the world, or Dick Woolf, who showed me how to be a trade unionist, democrat and communist.

Also, I would like to dedicate this collection to Jim Mortimer, whose friendship throughout most of my adult life has been hugely important. And to Rodney Bickerstaffe, an ever present and generous friend.

First and last I am a British trade unionist and proud of our history and my class. It has been the motive for my life's activity, like millions of others. It also led me to internationalism. Since retiring from trade union work, Cuba has been a great inspiration to me. On retirement from trade union work, I was invited to chair CSC, which is run by a dedicated team led by Rob Miller. Therefore my dedication must also include the heroic people of Cuba and their revolutionary leadership.

KGill

March 2009

ACKNOWLEDGEMENTS This collection of caricatures owes its title to a remark made by Rodney Bickerstaffe at Ken Gill's 80th birthday celebration at Congress House, see page 16. The editors would also like to thank the following individuals who have given this project their support: Ray Alderson, Vic Allen, Brendan Barber, Rodney Bickerstaffe, Albert Booth, Ken Cameron, Monire Childs, Christine Coates and James Goddard of London Metropolitan University, Andy Croft, Tony Dubbins, Tom and Joe Gill, Alan Jinkinson, Carolyn Jones, Jack and Mike Jones, Sian Jones of CWU, Susan Michie, Jim and Pat Mortimer, Bob Oram, Jim Pennington at Lithosphere, Malcolm Polfreman at Marx Memorial Library, Chris Proctor of ASLEF, Paul Routledge, Michael Seifert, Tom Sibley, Keith Sneddon, Graham Stevenson, Muss Sourani, Baroness Muriel Turner, Andrew Wiard.

Special thanks are due to Cliff Cocker for fine-tuning the text. And finally, of course, Norma and Ken Gill without whose full co-operation and support this project would not have come to fruition.

The editors plead guilty to supplying the text and accept full responsibility for any inaccuracies. However, any complaints about the veracity of the caricatures have to be laid at Ken's door alone.

Right: Roger Lyons looks suitably menacing as he ensures there are no suspicious characters loitering around this page

CONTENTS

Left: Roger Lyons, Macbeth-like, out to settle scores in the dead of night

KEN GILL – DRAWN TO STRUGGLE Ken Gill was born in 1927 in Melksham, Wiltshire, the son of a plumber cum shopkeeper and the youngest of four children.

During the Second World War, aged 16, he became an apprentice draughtsman after refusing to take up the offer of officer training open to grammar school boys. His decision, he says, was due to ideological opposition to the officer class. He was politicised early, having experienced poverty as a child during the Depression, and losing his older brother Leslie, an airman, during a raid over Germany.

During the war his family took as a lodger a boot-repairer and communist who turned the young Ken to the cause of socialism. At the time the Red Army was fighting the nazis at Stalingrad and Ken followed the war raging on the Eastern Front and celebrated victory in 1945. During that year, he was a prominent campaigner for the local Labour candidate who, as usual in a mainly rural Tory seat, was defeated.

Over the years, Ken became well known in union circles for his ability as a caricaturist. As a child his entry to a Daily Sketch children's art competition was disqualified because the judges didn't believe a child could produce a work of such

Left with Barbara Switzer at a TASS conference; **right** with Tony Benn

maturity. In those days, artistic talent in working class boys was not seen as a path to a creative career but to a seat in a drawing office and he duly served his time at a mechanical handling firm.

After divorcing his first wife Jacqueline, he married Tess Gill, a civil rights lawyer and leading figure in the British women's movement for many years. The couple had three children, Joe, Tom and Emma.

At the height of the Cold War, he travelled to East Germany for a youth congress and was arrested by the US military police. He was also in Paris during protests demanding Algerian independence when the police opened fire on demonstrators.

In his early thirties Ken became a director of a successful small engineering firm, proving his skills as a salesman and negotiator. Yet his involvement in trade unionism led him in a different direction and he was elected as a regional official of the Draughtsmen's and Allied Technicians' Association (DATA) in 1962. Posted to Liverpool, he was also made responsible for Northern Ireland.

The right-wing union leadership hoped this young militant would be ignominiously defeated by the intractable sectarian and anarchist problems endemic in the region during those years.

As a huge wave of industrial militancy swept both regions, Ken found himself leading workers in a series of battles over pay and conditions. His success as a persuasive, militant but shrewd official brought him to higher office in 1968, when he was elected deputy general secretary of the union.

In 1974, he became General Secretary of DATA's successor, TASS (Technical, Administrative and Supervisory Staffs Association), and later of MSF (Manufacturing, Science and Finance) following the merger with white collar union ASTMS.

During the 1980s Gill took the union through a series of mergers with other smaller craft and professional unions. By the time he retired in 1992, it had become a large multi-industry union; it was renamed Amicus and eventually became Unite.

In 1969, Ken spearheaded trade union opposition to In Place of Strife, Barbara Castle's contentious Bill on industrial relations and, five years later, was one of the leaders of the resistance to the Labour government's demand for a wage-restraining Social Contract.

Ken was on the TUC General Council for 18 years and a member of several of its sub-committees. In 1974, with over 7 million votes, he became the first communist to be elected on to the TUC General Council. With the election of other left-wingers, he helped lead a militant broad left grouping on the Council which spearheaded the ideological and economic battles during the seventies. He was one of a small number of General Council members who argued consistently for left policies during the 1970s and 1980s; his arguments and insistence on such policies were of crucial importance in the trade union movement as a whole.

Ken was not an isolated figure on the TUC, but he was the most ideologically committed in a group of left wing union leaders including miners' leader Lawrence Daly, Rodney

Top left: in Havana with Fidel Castro; **top right:** with Nelson Mandela; **left:** with T&G General Secretary Bill Morris, T&G South Eastern Region Secretary Barry Camfield and Gordon Brown

Bickerstaffe of Nupe, Alan Sapper of the film workers and the 'terrible twins', Hugh Scanlon and Jack Jones.

There were fears within the Labour Party that this new militant trade unionism would undermine government, while in the establishment and security services it was believed the unions were threatening to undermine the capitalist system as a whole. Prime Minister Harold Wilson alluded to leaders like Gill when he spoke of 'a tightly knit group of politically motivated men' out to undermine democracy.

During the miner's strike of 1984 TASS assisted the NUM and Ken's union faced possible sequestration of funds for falling foul of the Thatcher government's ban on solidarity action.

Within the TUC he fought for more progressive positions internationally and for the unions to support anti-racist positions within the movement itself. Thus Ken and his union were among the earliest supporters of the fight against South African apartheid and on his initiative, the union guaranteed the deposit for the Wembley stadium concert that celebrated Mandela's 70th birthday while he was still in jail on Robben Island.

Left with Mikhail Gorbachev; **top right** with Neil Kinnock and Clive Jenkins; **right** with Harold Pinter

This was acknowledged by Mandela when, on his first UK visit, he chose the union's conference hall to meet and thank ANC exiles and activists.

While Ken could be forceful and committed, he was never dogmatic or unnecessarily aggressive. He was tall, with a rugged handsomeness and his soft Wiltshire drawl and ready laughter belied his steely determination. He was always a popular member of the General Council even if the colour of his politics weren't. In 1993 he was voted the 'Trade Unionists' Trade Unionist' in a survey carried out by the Observer newspaper.

He was a trade unionist through and through, believing them to be the necessary basis of any radical social change. But he also believed that the Labour Party was central to such change.

Retirement from full-time union work in 1992 didn't, however, mean withdrawing to a country retreat or a seat in the House of Lords. He continued campaigning on radical issues, marching and speaking out against the Iraq war, right up until his illness confined him to home. He was particularly keen on promoting solidarity with Cuba – for over a decade, he was Chair of the Cuba Solidarity Campaign and met Cuba's leader Fidel Castro on several occasions.

After separating from Tess he married Norma Bramley, a politically active headteacher, with whom he still lives. He will be remembered as someone who turned a medium-sized craft union into a large militant one; he was an outstanding leader of the struggle to save British manufacturing, often fighting virtually alone.

Ken was always a determined and passionately committed internationalist and has been a prominent campaigner and organiser for the anti-apartheid movement.

He will long be remembered for his consistent opposition to an imposed and restrictive incomes policy, whether by Conservative or Labour governments.

Sources Spycatcher by Peter Wright; The Secret War Against the Miners by Seamus Milne; The Three Pillars of Liberty by Francesca Klug, Keir Starmer and Stuart Weir.

Top Ken Gill, centre, having a ball with two legends of the trade union movement, miners' leader Mick McGahey and T&G General Secretary, and later National Pensioners Convention leader, Jack Jones; **above** Ken, left, with John Prescott, Rodney Bickerstaffe and former FBU General Secretary Ken Cameron; **left** the magnificent 12, standing l to r Alan Tuffin, Alan Sapper, unknown, Geoffrey Drain, Ken Gill, Norman Willis, unknown, Hugh Scanlon; crouching: Ken Cameron, Bill Sirs, Terry Duffy and Moss Evans

INTRODUCTION When it comes to the luck of the draw, Ken Gill has it. It's one thing to have a great, if quirky sense of humour. It's quite another to be able to get quickly to the core of an issue, to the essence of a personality or to point up some trait. But Ken's supreme gift is to draw a cartoon which invariably pleases the 'target' and amuses everyone else. In these images, old friends are returned to us, past times brought to mind, the famous gently mocked – and the pompous deflated. Like the craftsmen and craftswomen he represented for decades, his own skills were honed over years of apprenticeship and work as an engineering draughtsman. But the cartoons are pure Ken, and like the man himself, always a delight. Draw your own conclusions!

Rodney Bickerstaffe

Rodney Bickerstaffe demonstrates a unique interpretation of true brotherly love in this attempt to throttle Clive Jenkins

Thumbs down from Roger Lyons

THE CARICATURES

TONY BENN formerly Second Viscount Stansgate is an indefatigable fighter for socialism and undoubtedly the most revered and best-known left-wing politician in Britain. Renowned as perhaps the best political speaker the left has, Benn is never without his beloved pipe, which must be stuffed with some socialist strain of marijuana – the more he smokes, the more radical he becomes!

In the second Wilson government (1966-70) he was Minister of Technology and in the third (1974-76) he initially served as Secretary of State for Industry before being transferred to Secretary of State for Energy.

In the 1970s and 1980s, he was the most prominent figure on the left of the parliamentary Labour Party and the term 'Bennite' (never used by Benn himself) came to denote someone on the left of the party.

During his time as Secretary of State for Industry he was instrumental in supporting the establishment of worker co-operatives at Standard Triumph in Coventry and Fisher-Bendix in Liverpool, where workers had taken over their factories to avoid closure and redundancies.

While Benn enjoyed prominence in the political hierarchy, he was demonised by the mainstream press as the most dangerous man in Britain. His suppport for the labour movement and unshakable belief in socialism was feared by the establishment. Once he had been successfully marginalised from the power structures, he began to enjoy dubious renown among his foes who now treat him with a condescending and reluctant admiration for his integrity.

He left parliament in 2001 'to spend more time in politics,' as he quipped, tongue in cheek.

Questions he says should to be asked of anyone in power are:

❝ What power have you got? Where did you get it from? In whose interests do you use it? To whom are you accountable? How do we get rid of you? ❞

RODNEY BICKERSTAFFE was General Secretary of Britain's largest public service trade union UNISON until 2001.

He was dubbed 'the Buddy Holly of the trade union movement' for his large, dark-rimmed glasses and his quiff of hair, reminiscent of the American rock-and-roll pioneer.

Bickerstaffe became an organiser for the National Union of Public Employees (NUPE) in 1966 in Yorkshire, rising through the ranks to be divisional officer of the northern division. Bickerstaffe was elected general secretary in November 1995.

He was a popular and highly-visible trade union leader, always passionate in his campaigns, particularly those against low pay and he played a large part in ensuring the overdue introduction of a statutory national minimum wage by a Labour government in 1999.

When he retired from UNISON in 2001 he took no paid employment and refused a seat in the House of Lords.

In 2001 he succeeded Jack Jones as president of the National Pensioners Convention. He chairs the Global Network which works with organisations in Asia, Africa and Latin America and is President of War on Want.

At the 2004 Labour Party Conference Tony Blair made reference to Bickerstaffe during his speech, at which point booing broke out. 'That's funny,' he quipped, 'I thought no one booed Rodney Bickerstaffe.' Of course they hadn't – they were booing because at that moment 82-year-old Walter Wolfgang was being ejected from the hall for heckling Blair! Teflon Tony's comment was a reflection of Bickerstaffe's popularity.

He will be remembered as someone who never veered from his course of highlighting the situation of the under-paid in the public services, particularly women, and fighting unstintingly for their just treatment.

At Ken's 80th birthday celebrations at the TUC Rodney in his address said:

" we all knew Ken was good at drawing and there were a number of trade union leaders who would have loved to see Ken drawn too, but only after he'd been hung and quartered! "

I DID BUT SEE HIM
PASSING BY...

ALBERT BOOTH was Secretary of State for Employment in Prime Minister Callaghan's cabinet from 1976 to 1979. He was a Labour Party politician from South Shields who became a design draughtsman and joined Ken Gill's union, TASS. He was MP for Barrow-in-Furness from 1966 to 1983.

Albert was a committed and active member of CND and his opposition to the Polaris nuclear submarine programme cost him his seat when, after boundary changes, it fell to the Conservatives. When Trident was launched in Barrow by the Queen, he wrote an article in his union journal: 'Why I will not be there.' His opposition to nuclear weapons was always highly principled.

Booth was made Secretary of State for Employment in Prime Minister Callaghan's cabinet and performed the task from 1976 to 1979. He was known as 'Foot's favourite son'.

Booth and Foot represented that very short-lived period, in the late 70s and early 80s, when the Labour Party had moved to the left and there was hope for a government really representing working people and with genuine socialist policies.'

Ken recalls: 'Albert Booth and Michael Foot were two of the few honourable ministers in the Callaghan government one could negotiate with, trust and respect. Foot was straight in his dealings with the trade union movement and both Booth and the then Labour Party General Secretary, Jim Mortimer, maintained a close liaison with the unions.'

Booth remembers when:

❝ Ken was TASS district organiser in Liverpool, he was so good at encouraging members to put in claims to improve their terms and conditions that the union was obliged to employ a new officer, Len Formby, to deal with them. In one workplace, to force the issue, the workers began a 'go slow'. The boss complained to Len that this was not allowed under the procedural agreement. Len vehemently denied that it was a go-slow. 'What the hell is it then?' asked the irate manager. 'It's working without enthusiasm', Len replied laconically. ❞

JOHN BOYD was a Salvation Army officer, played in one of its bands and epitomised the caricature image of a Scottish Presbyterian – dour, moralising and intolerant.

He became General Secretary of the Amalgamated Union of Engineering Workers (AUEW) Engineering Section in 1975 when the union lurched to the right after Hugh Scanlon retired.

He held extremely right-wing views and hated everyone on the left, including Scanlon. In the seventies the 'terrible twins' (Jack Jones and Hugh Scanlon) led the two most powerful unions in the country and this was a time when the employers and right wing political leaders quaked in their shoes.

A massive campaign was unleashed in the mainstream press to vilify the left in the unions and to engineer the re-installation of right-wingers who would be loyal to the capitalist class. With Boyd's election, their aims began to be fulfilled.

Boyd, together with Terry Duffy and later with Eric Hammond and Frank Chapple of the ETU formed the reinstalled right wing of the British trade union movement and after the AEU finally achieved a merger with the electricians union gave great solace to the employers and governments of the period.

The Roberts Arundel strike which ran for 18 bitter months from 1967 to 1968 became a touchstone in the battle between intransigent bosses and unions. Engineering workers struck against their American dyed-in-the-wool anti-union boss, William Pomeranz, who owned the Roberts Arundel textile machine factory in Stockport.

Boyd was the national union official responsible for this dispute. He was a candidate for the AEU presidency at the time and claimed at one point to be close to persuading Mr Pomeranz to agree to most of the union's demands. But he disappeared from the scene after the agreement mysteriously collapsed and was later accused of using the strike to further his own popularity.

When Scanlon accepted a peerage, Boyd momentarily lost his rag and whined:

    They only gave me a knighthood and they give that damned commie a peerage!

LEONID BREZHNEV (1906-1982) was General Secretary of the Soviet Communist Party. He held that office longer than anyone other than Joseph Stalin and recent polls showed him to have been the most popular Russian leader of the twentieth century.

Brezhnev might not have been a very charismatic figure but the period of his leadership saw a thaw in the Cold War and gave everyone hope for a future of peace and détente. The Helsinki Declaration in 1975 on Security and Cooperation in Europe provided the continent with a blueprint for genuine peaceful co-existence after years of aggressive posturing and with the world continually on the brink of nuclear war.

'I had always been a supporter of the USSR and remained convinced of its unique role in defeating European fascism and in the destruction of the colonial empires,' Ken recalls.

He remembers being in Moscow in the eighties at a trade union conference and speaking about the impact of technology and how it could help overcome bureaucracy.

'I said that I had heard the Soviet Union suffered particularly from this problem and my comments were given front page coverage in Pravda. This made me the centre of media attention.'

When Brezhnev spoke at the conference, Ken decided to sketch him and was filmed doing this by a Russian TV crew.

Ken relates:

66 I met my interpreter of that time years later, after the demise of the Soviet Union. She told me she'd been given a thorough talking-to after the shot of me making a sketch of Brezhnev was shown, and was told that she should have stopped me doing this; she was even threatened with losing her job. 99

'This was a sign of the humour deficit and rigidity which characterised the restrictive climate of the period, and was associated with the growing stagnation in Soviet economic and political life', he says.

RAY BUCKTON (1922-1995) was a prominent trade unionist from Yorkshire. He was General Secretary of the train drivers' union, the Associated Society of Locomotive Engineers and Firemen (Aslef 1970-87) and a member of the TUC General Council from 1973 to 1986.

A convinced socialist, Ray was leader of the train drivers' union during some of the labour movement's most tempestuous years. When rail passengers vented their spleen after waiting on cold platforms during periods of industrial action, he accepted that, as general secretary, he was paid to take the abuse.

His was the face and the voice of the union and the vitriol of the national media was targeted at him, but he was admired within the labour movement as a staunch trade unionist and defender of his members.

Ray was larger than life. He was a gregarious, amiable man who loved a drink and a chat with anyone who wished to speak to him, and singsongs after union conferences were never complete without his mouth-organ accompaniment.

And he had a great sense of humour. Seriously ill in hospital, he was visited by a union official he disliked and so pretended to be asleep, feigning snoring. He opened his eyes only when the unwelcome visitor had left. 'I thought that bugger would never go,' he told the nurse.

But as a trade union leader, Ray was never the type to hide and he always faced the flak when the going got rough. He was also a passionate opponent of the South African apartheid regime and a leading figure in the British-Soviet Friendship Society.

During times of industrial action he and his wife Barbara suffered death threats, violence, broken windows, abusive telephone calls and poison-pen letters, not to mention filth pushed through their letter-box and a commuter writing to inform him that he was the 'greatest traitor since Guy Fawkes'

But though in the media's eyes he was a left-wing ogre, it was typical of Ray that he maintained a close friendship with a number of industrial correspondents.

JAMES CALLAGHAN (1912–2005) was leader of the Labour Party from 1976 to 1980, Prime Minister from 1976 to 1979 and ended up as Baron Callaghan of Cardiff. Commonly known as Sunny Jim, Gentleman Jim, Big Jim or just plain Jim. Callaghan is the only politician to date who has served in all four of the great offices of state as Prime Minister, Chancellor of the Exchequer, Foreign and Home Secretaries.

Like many others, he was a firm supporter of the left early in his political life before moving in the opposite direction in order to further his career in the Labour Party. An example of just how far he was prepared to go is related by QC John Platts-Mills. In his autobiography he tells how, as a confirmed teetotaller, Callaghan patriotically glugged down the vodka toasts on a visit to Moscow in 1945 in order to uphold the honour of the British delegation. After staggering back to Britain, he apparently never touched a drop again.

The Labour Party lost the general election in 1970, but Callaghan returned to office as Foreign Secretary in March 1974, taking responsibility for renegotiating the terms of the United Kingdom's membership of the European Economic Community, and supporting a Yes vote for Britain remaining in the organisation in the 1975 referendum.

When Wilson resigned in 1976, Callaghan was elected the new Labour leader.

Caught between the rock of industrial disputes and widespread strikes during the much-publicised 'Winter of Discontent' of 1978–79 and the hard place of a capitalist system with its real underlying problems, Sunny Jim's chronic indecision made his government increasingly inefficient and unpopular and helped bring his party's subsequent defeat by the Tories in national elections in 1979, bringing Margaret Thatcher to power. His incapability of addressing the justified anger of low-paid public sector workers, but instead kow-towing to the IMF, lost his government any credibility and goodwill it had once enjoyed.

Ken remembers:

❝ **When Callaghan approached me after some heavy negotiations and said: 'I have an offer to make, why don't you just take up cartooning full-time so that we can get on with our work in peace'!** ❞

KEN CAMERON was General Secretary of the FBU from 1980 until 2000 and presided over the longest period of stability in the fire service since the national strike of 1972. This was an achievement that owed much to his ability to get along with politicians of every hue.

Describing him as 'The Mr. Punch lookalike of the Labour Movement,' Mirror journalist Paul Routledge relates that at union conferences Ken would on occasions look at the clock and then say to his colleagues: 'It's now one o'clock Moscow time, so it's time for the pub.'

On his retirement, Ken Cameron's successor as general secretary of the FBU Andy Gilchrist wrote in The Firefighter: 'Ken is a unique individual. There are many, many complimentary things to be said about him – a man whose heart and soul are rooted in the struggle against injustice, intolerance and inequality. The test of a leader is the legacy he leaves behind'.

'Ken has safeguarded the future of the FBU by leaving a healthy lay democracy in place and a union committed to the principles of peace and progress'

He was a great help to the miners during the big 1984-85 strike and tells how on one occasion he accompanied Arthur Scargill's driver to collect £200,000 in cash from the Co-op Bank.

He told the understandably inquisitive chief teller they needed the money because they'd been given a good tip on a gee-gee. 'And', Ken added: 'he didn't even ask us for its name!'

FRANK CHAPPLE (1921-2004) joined the Electrical Trades Union (ETU) in 1937 and the Communist Party in 1939. In 1947 he and Leslie Cannon represented the ETU at a conference of the communist World Federation of Democratic Youth in Prague, but in subsequent years he became a visceral anti-communist.

He was the archetypical East End 'Barra Boy' with his greased hair and cheeky-chappie sly grin. Not the sort of bloke you'd want to buy a second hand car from.

Without his early training in the Communist Party he would hardly have made it beyond shop steward, but the needs of the Cold War allowed much dross to rise to the surface and he was propelled to undreamt of prominence.

He was general secretary of the ETU (later EEPTU) from 1966 to 1984 before his retirement when he was appointed to the House of Lords as Lord Chapple of Hoxton.

Paul Routledge says: '...he learned the tricks of the trade in the Communist Party and then put them to brilliant use to oust his former comrades. He was uncompromising in his jihad against the Left'.

Ken tells the story of when he was with Chapple in the USA as a member of a TUC delegation under the leadership of TUC General Secretary Len Murray:

“In Arizona we found ourselves talking to a real redneck union official whose office wall was adorned with guns and who regaled us with blood-curdling stories about how US unions dealt with 'Commies'. For obvious reasons, I kept my mouth shut. I left as quickly as I could and was relieved to sink back into the seat of the limousine placed at our disposal. Frank Chapple jumped in beside me 'Fank God for dat,' he said, 'I faught for a mo' you was going to admit being a commie and e'd 'ave shot the bloody lot of us!'”

A visual quote from John Heartfield's famous Spirit of Geneva 1932 poster of a bayonetted dove, exposing Germany's rearmament as a threat to peace

MIKKI DOYLE (1916-1995), born Miriam Leventhal in New York of East European Jewish parents, was the Women's Editor of the Morning Star in the days when it had one. 'When the feminist movement started the Women's Pages of Britain's press were full of the usual shopping, fashion and cosmetics crap,' she said. 'We got rid of all that.'

She was an important participant in founding Women in Media, an organisation which had a lasting effect on contemporary journalism. Her close relationships with 'female comrades' as she put it, ranging from the radical Guardian journalist Jill Tweedie to the devout Catholic the Marchioness of Lothian, were typical of her capacity to 'embrace everyone with a good heart'.

In 1949 she met and married the Glasgow-born Communist Charlie Doyle. He was her one-way ticket to Britain when he became the first deportee under the McCarran Act. McCarthy purges had taken him from the leadership of the Gas, Coke and Chemical Workers Union to an Ellis Island prison. Mikki married him by proxy while he was in jail, then came with him to London.

Her long friendship with Claudia Jones, perhaps the most brilliant black Communist activist of her generation, profoundly influenced her.

Ken remembers: 'when Charlie Doyle died, I gave the funeral oration. I was fond of him and I felt very emotional. After making my speech I got down from the podium and stood next to Mikki, completely drained. Then, from behind her hand and in a very loud stage whisper, she said to me: "Press the fucking button!" I'd forgotten it was my duty, once I'd finished, to send Charlie's coffin on its way.'

She was an inveterate chain-smoker and while on the New York subway was desperate for a fag, so lit up in the subway entrance. Around her were the prostrate bodies of sleeping homeless. A young woman carefully stepped over these bodies to approach her and tell her she shouldn't be smoking. Mikki rounded on her and said:

> **Why don't you bloody well show some fucking concern about the homeless lying here rather than me having an innocent fag!**

TONY DUBBINS was Assistant General Secretary of the National Graphical Association (NGA) in the late 1970s. He succeeded Joe Wade as General Secretary in 1984 and remained in this post for 24 years.

He was President of the TUC (1997) and was the longest serving member of the General Council – 23 years – what prison officers call a life sentence.

The early eighties saw the start of Thatcher's attacks on the unions, and the print workers bore much of the brunt of these. In the Eddie Shah/Stockport Messenger dispute in Warrington, the new Tory laws were used for the first time against trade unions. During this dispute the NGA faced sequestration of its assets in defence of its members.

Tony Dubbins led the Wapping dispute which was, along with the miners' strike of 1984-5, one of the key turning points in the history of the trade union movement in Britain.

It started in 1986 when around 6,000 newspaper workers went on strike after Rupert Murdoch's News International tried to introduce new technology and with it drastically change the contract of their employees for the worse.

The defeat of the print workers in Wapping meant a serious weakening of the print unions nationally. The NGA eventually merged into Amicus, following a period of mergers within the print industry in which he emerged as the elected leader.

Tony was also very supportive of other unions. During the miners' strike, for example, the NGA gave crucial assistance to the NUM.

Shortly after the Berlin Wall came down the Financial Times transferred printing of its German addition from West Germany to a printing company in the former East Germany. The employer refused to recognise the national agreements of the German Print Union IG Medien and a dispute ensued.

They soon found themselves short of skilled printers and advertised in the Daily Mail for British printers.

Tony Dubbins recalls what followed:

> After contacting our German sister union, two of our Executive members and my personal assistant, all skilled printers, applied for the jobs with both union´s approval. They were flown out, all expenses paid, got the jobs and were due to start work the following Monday. Then they crossed the picket line to a cacaphony of boos. Once inside they quickly persuaded the workers in the plant to join the strike halting production imediately. In no time a full agreement for recognition with the German print union was signed.

TERRY DUFFY (1922-85) succeeded Hugh Scanlon in 1978 as president of the Amalgamated Engineering Union (AEU). He was another figure who would hardly have progressed beyond the lower trade union echelons if it hadn't been for the Cold War.

As the right tightened its grip on this key union, Duffy, a visceral anti-communist, attacked Gill and other left wing trade unionists whenever he had the opportunity. Under the right wing trinity of Duffy, Laird and Jordan, the AEU became one of the few unions the Labour leadership could count on in its battles with the left in the union movement.

Duffy was also happy to go along with Thatcher's new industrial relations laws, which demanded that unions officially register to be 'protected' under the legislation. TUC policy was that unions should not register, but the right-wing-led ETU was the first to renege on this and was duly followed by the AEU. Gill called for their expulsion from the TUC, but the call was not taken up.

A measure of Duffy is that he once told Roy Hattersley: 'I hate that Jim Mortimer' (who was the then General Secretary of the Labour Party and a principled left-winger).

Hattersley asked him why, expecting a diatribe about Mortimer's left-wing views.

'Well, he's a bloody draughtsman,' Duffy replied – a sad reflection of narrow-mindedness by a former shop-floor worker to those who worked in the office, even though most of them, like Mortimer, had themselves started out on the shop-floor.

Ian McGregor, Thatcher's hatchet man at the Coal Board during the infamous 1984/5 strike heaped praise on right wing union leaders like Duffy in his memoirs. It was not widely known at the time to what extent these union leaders had cooperated with McGregor throughout the strike. He says:

John Boyd of the engineers was one of my most important confidants on union matters... Through him I also had come to know and respect the AUEW president Terry Duffy, for whom I had as much regard. In fact, there were a number of trade union leaders with whom I could talk frankly – including Gavin Laird, Gerry Eastwood, Alan Tuffin... and of course, Frank Chapple.

JOHN EDMONDS was General Secretary of the General, Municipal and Boilermakers' Union (GMB) from 1986 to 2003

He was the son of a shop steward and became a keen cricketer and cabinet-maker. He went to Oriel College, Oxford and was one of the few university-educated union leaders at the time.

He helped build the GMB into what became Britain's third largest union, securing re-election in 1991 and 1996. He became one of Tony Blair's most vociferous critics in the trade union movement after the latter's election as Labour leader and gained notoriety as one of the prominent trade unionists branded 'wreckers' by government ministers for attempting to block the privatisation of public services. He argued that using private finance was costly to the public purse and undermined the principle of public service.

In an apparent fit of pique and out of character, he played a crucial role in the heavy defeat for Tony Blair over public-private partnerships at the Labour Party conference in 2001, insisting that 'we have to put a marker down for ministers.' The GMB also cut its financial support to the Labour Party by £500,000 annually and criticised political funding by major private donors.

He oversaw the opening of a GMB office in Brussels, the first British union to open one there, and criticised Blair for not backing Britain's entry into the single currency more vigorously.

66 When he served as President of the TUC in 1998, The Guardian published his photograph on the front page, alongside his outspoken comments about the 'greedy bastards' (of the City). These comments should be considered visionary and if made today would win plaudits rather than opprobrium. What a difference a decade makes. 99

MICHAEL FOOT with his long hair, glasses and duffle coat was sometimes portrayed, unfairly, as the dotty intellectual. But this caricature went down well in Britain's anti-intellectual climate and served to mask the validity of his profound socialist convictions.

In 1963 he became the leader of Labour's left opposition from the back benches, dazzling the Commons with his well-honed rhetoric.

Foot was a founder member of the Campaign for Nuclear Disarmament, opposed the Vietnam war, and denounced Soviet suppression of 'socialism with a human face' in Czechoslovakia in 1968.

When Labour returned to office in March 1974 under Harold Wilson, Foot became Secretary of State for Employment and in this role he played the major part in government efforts to keep the trade unions on side. He was also responsible for introducing the Health and Safety at Work Act.

Following the defeat of Labour by Margaret Thatcher in 1979, Foot was elected Labour leader the following year, beating the right's candidate Denis Healey.

The 1983 Labour Manifesto, strongly socialist in tone, pledged abolition of the House of Lords, nationalisation of the banks, unilateral nuclear disarmament and higher personal taxation

But in 1983, under his leadership, the Labour Party lost to the Conservatives in a landslide and he resigned as leader and was succeeded by Neil Kinnock.

According to Ken when Foot was Secretary of State for Employment, together with the Labour Party General Secretary Jim Mortimer, new industrial legislation and protections for trade unions were under discussion and agreement was reached on all key issues.

Foot has been a dedicated supporter of Plymouth Argyle F.C. since childhood, and served for several years as a director of the club:

" **For his 90th birthday present in 2003 the club registered him as a player and gave him the shirt number 90. This made him the oldest registered player in the history of football. He has stated that he will not 'conk out' until he has seen his team play in the Premiership!** "

JOE GORMLEY (1917 –1993), later Baron Gormley OBE, was President of the National Union of Mineworkers from 1971 to 1982 when he was replaced by Arthur Scargill. Brought up a strict Catholic, he was a blunt Lancastrian – full of bluster and banter but little substance.

He presided over the big miners' strike of 1972, which lasted for seven weeks during which emergency measures were used to economise on electricity by reducing the working week to three days. After hard negotiation, the strike was resolved with greatly increased pay and concessions won by the miners.

Two years later, the miners voted again for strike action which started in February 1974. Edward Heath called a snap election on the issue, asking the public to decide over whether unions had too much power. He lost and Labour won.

'I come from a rough school', he wrote in his autobiography Battered Cherub, recalling a time when he and some other right-wing leaders were jostled outside the NUM offices by Scottish miners. Seeing their leftwing leaders Mick McGahey and Bill McClain in the foyer he relates that he: 'played holy hell with the pair of them …you're responsible when you bring people down…I'm telling you if it happens again I'll bring a few dozen Lancashire lads down and we'll bloody sort the lot of you out'.

He also described himself as '…enjoying the odd pint or two, and I don't suppose there's much secret over the years that I like the horses and I like a good meal.' On one occasion he tried to persuade the union to invest in a race horse but the project died after he was made a laughing stock in the press.

> **During 2002 there were allegations that Gormley had worked for Special Branch by passing information on so-called extremists within his own union.**

An anonymous witness, claiming to be a Special Branch officer, said Gormley did this because '…he loved his country; he was a patriot and very worried about the growth of militancy within his own union.' He was always a 'moderate' leader in a union noted for its militancy.

GEORGE GUY (1918– 2005) was the last leader of the National Union of Sheet Metal, Copper, Heating and Domestic Engineers, one of the craft unions formed in the early days of the industrial revolution.

He became general secretary in 1974 and retired after the merger with TASS in 1985. He was elected to the general council of the TUC, where he played a strong role in the difficult days of Thatcherism and TUC cautiousness. Under his leadership, the union merged with Ken Gill's union, TASS. He served on the TUC General Council from 1977-1983 and was a member of the Engineering Industry Training Board from 1977 until 1984.

George was proud to be an engineer and proud to be a trade unionist. He believed workers could better themselves through solidarity with each other.

> His childhood in London's East End meant that he had been surrounded by immigrants, mostly Jewish, who, he claimed, gave him his special accent as well as his cryptic, sardonic humour and his instinctive anti-racism and internationalism.

He learned his engineering skills as an apprentice in a North London factory in the 1930s and it was there he became a trade union activist. Over the next twenty years he applied both his talents as an engineer and his energy as a union activist, eventually becoming a full time official.

George had robust class instincts and loyalties which were reflected in his judgements and conduct throughout his long life in the labour movement. He was the first to offer solidarity and help to other sections of workers in struggle in Britain and he was an uncompromising ally of the miners and the print workers in their fight back against the Thatcherite onslaught.

As a communist, he was naturally an internationalist. He was a supporter of the Soviet Union and was saddened deeply by its collapse.

He was an anti-racist and anti-imperialist. His union signed up to the anti-apartheid and anti-colonial movements from the outset, in contrast to the last-minute conversions of some in the labour movement.

KGⅢ 82

ERIC HAMMOND was General Secretary of the EEPTU from 1984-92. Despising the Left, he formed a ready alliance with fellow electrician Frank Chapple and with John Boyd and Bill Jordan of the AUEW, as part of the 'Ermine Hotel Group (named after the hotel where they regularly met).

In league with the employers who wanted to 'rationalise' industrial relations and deal only with one union, he proposed the ETU as a 'business union', strike-free and party to 'sweetheart' deals with the employers.

While at Tolpuddle, Ken was chairing a meeting on trade union negotiations at the government spy headquarters of GCHQ, when he found himself having to defend Hammond's right to speak in the face of hostile heckling by workers who had no love for Hammond's policies.

But Hammond sometimes showed a paranoid fear about the influence of the left.

Rodney Bickerstaffe relates that Ken Gill was instrumental in putting his name forward as a candidate to become chair of the important TUC economic committee: 'There was a knife-edge vote as many leaders were not keen to let a left-winger take on the chair of this committee. Eric Hammond, who was in the north of England at his union's conference, was determined to ensure I didn't get elected.'

" Hammond had to get up extremely early in the morning in order to arrive in London in time to cast his vote against me. However the train was delayed and he arrived just after the vote had been taken. He was livid and went up to Jimmy Knapp (then leader of the railworkers' union RMT) and said: 'Admit it, your lot did this on purpose, deliberately delaying my train!' "

BRANCHING OUT INTO NEW UNIONISM

JOHN HAYLETT, Morning Star editor from 1995 to 2008, hails from Liverpool and joined the Communist Party in 1963 aged 18. Moving to London the following year, he worked for ten years at British Telecom's international telephone exchange, becoming an activist and then local and regional lay official for the Union of Post Office Workers, now the Communication Workers' Union.

He was also a leading activist in a number of anti-imperialist struggles, particularly in the anti-apartheid movement during the seventies and eighties.

After gaining a degree in Modern Languages and Economic Studies at Newcastle Polytechnic (now the University of Northumbria) in 1981, he joined the Morning Star as a news reporter in February 1983 and was appointed editor in April 1995.

He took on the editorship of the Morning Star at one of its most crtitical moments. When the Communist Party split in the eighties, the Democratic Left faction attempted to assert its control over the paper, but was defeated. John and his fellow journalists kept the paper going, despite the Jeremiahs predicting its imminent demise. He has been instrumental in transforming it into a paper that, while remained loyal to its trade union base, has opened up its pages to a wide range of opinion from the broad left.

After nearly 14 years as editor, he stepped down at the end of 2008, taking up the post of political editor. He now lives for much of his time in Cardiff.

A passionate supporter of Everton FC, he has 'tha Scouser's' gift of repartee and a dry sense of humour.

To keep up spirits in Morning Star's editorial office in times of crisis the Scouser in John would take over with sardonic lines like:

66 **When things seem like they can't get worse, they probably will, so press on rewardless.** 99

DENNIS HEALEY, later Baron Healey, was nicknamed Dennis the Menace. He was Secretary of State for Defence from 1964-1970 and Chancellor of the Exchequer from 1974-1979. Born in Leeds, he was elected to the House of Commons for Leeds South East in 1952. He had been a member of the Communist Party for a short period in 1937 while a student at Oxford, but he soon moved rightwards and was a chief supporter of the so-called moderates in the Labour Party .

In a speech in February 1974, Healey promised that he would 'tax the rich until the pips squeak' and the next month became Chancellor of the Exchequer after the Labour Party's election victory.

His decision, taken in conjunction with Prime Minister James Callaghan to seek an International Monetary Fund (IMF) loan and submit the British economy to the associated IMF supervision, ushered in cuts in public spending and wage control. It was widely regarded as a betrayal of Labour principles.

Healey's gritty persona and ready wit earned him wide popularity with the public. When the media were not present, his humour was equally caustic but more risqué. 'These fallacies (pronounced "phalluses") are rising up everywhere', he once remarked at a meeting of Leeds University Labour Society.

But one of his more amusing comments was in 1978, when he likened being attacked by the mild-mannered Sir Geoffrey Howe in the House of Commons to being 'savaged by a dead sheep.'

Ken met Healey on a number of occasions during trade union negotiations with the government. On one of these occasions, Ken relates:

" A TUC delegation had been negotiating with Callaghan and Healey at No.10 on wages and the government's proposed wage freeze, I needed to make an urgent phone call to my office. After the meeting finished, I asked Callaghan if I could use the phone. "Go ahead,' said the prime minister, 'use the one in the corridor.' While I am on the phone, I feel a light tap on my shoulder and, turning round, see it is Healey. He whispers to me: 'Reporting to Bert Ramelson* are we?' "

* Ramelson, see page 86, was the legendary and tough Industrial Organiser of the Communist Party and was well known to Healey from his own days in the CP.

TOM JACKSON (1925–2003) was known more for his spectacular handlebar moustache and ebullient personality than any reputation as a firebrand.

He was first elected to the Union of Postal Workers (UPW) executive council in 1955, seen then as a radical in a union with a long anti-Communist tradition.

He became General Secretary of the union in 1967 and remained in post for 17 years. The union, certainly not known for its militancy, was catapulted into its first national strike in 1971, something Jackson hardly envisaged happening. The strike, by 230,000 workers, brought him to public prominence. Postal workers' pay, already at the lower end of the scale, had been eroded by inflation and the members decided enough was enough. The strike, unlike those in many other sectors, enjoyed much public sympathy.

It was also the first time a national union had consciously used publicity in the mainstream press to advertise its members' grievances and why they were striking. The campaign was designed by Ken Sprague and Solly Kaye. This no doubt helped increase public support.

Later, he was widely criticised for risking an all-out strike at a time when the government had staked its future on holding down pay, and had put in a tough new boss at the Post Office. Jackson insisted it was the only option. His members wanted it.

He also predicted that the break-up of the old GPO would lead to the privatisation of telecommunications.

As the era of Margaret Thatcher's premiership dawned in 1979, Jackson found himself defending not only the integrity of the GPO, but also the Post Office's monopoly against Industry Secretary Sir Keith Joseph. He won that battle, but his attempt to prevent the privatisation of British Telecom was doomed.

Quoting Dorothy Parker in his valedictory conference address, he said, 'Don't think it hasn't been fun, because it hasn't been.'

Jackson always described himself as 'just a postman in a suit' was held in great affection by the great majority of his membership. They saw him as their first leader to raise their standing in public esteem.

FRED JARVIS was General Secretary of the National Union of Teachers (NUT) from 1975 to 1989.

His attitudes on social issues were progressive, but otherwise he was politically on the right – he even defended corporal punishment, a retrograde attitude which inspired the caricature.

Remembering the good old days, he tells how he greeted Prime Minister Macmillan at an NUT conference in 1963. The union had invited Macmillan to talk at conference because those were the days when secretaries of state and even prime ministers addressed NUT gatherings.

But it happened to be the day the Profumo scandal broke. Jarvis was fretting about how to greet Super Mac. Should he say: 'How is your day going?' or perhaps 'have you had a good day?' but he eventually opted for the simple, 'Hello Mr Macmillan. How are you?' To which the prime minister replied: 'Get me a Scotch.'

Ken's caricature has its roots in a rather bizarre story that created quite a stir in 1981. The Society of Teachers Opposed to Physical Punishment (STOPP) asked Jarvis to ban offending adverts for canes in the union's journal, The Teacher.

A group backed by leading educationalists claimed the advertiser had more sinister motives. He was a Bognor newsagent, who also advertised his canes in soft-porn magazines.

The controversy, as reported in The Times, developed into a spanking good row spiced with the threat of legal action.

66 Jarvis's passion was photgraphy and he took many pictures at pivotal moments in the history of the Labour Party. Blair referred to him as 'the Labour movement's very own paparazzo'. He was the only photographer allowed free access to Labour's Millbank HQ. 'Jarvis's pictures are a fascinating record of Teflon Tone's salad days'. 99

CLIVE JENKINS was General Secretary of ASTMS (the Association of Scientific, Technical and Managerial Staffs) from 1969 to 1988. Born in Port Talbot, south Wales, he was a genial Welshman with a sharp sense of humour and his politics were, if sometimes erratic, of the left. Without doubt, as a young trade union leader he was unique, committed and talented.

He was a favourite of the media for his ebullient personality and invariably witty responses to questions. In his Who's Who entry he gave 'Organising the middle classes' as his recreational activity. This sums up both his sense of humour and his achievement bringing professional workers into the British trade union movement. His was a largely white collar union and included many highly paid scientific and professional workers.

In later life, Clive Jenkins became an avid environmentalist and one of his chief interests was campaigning to save whales – hence the caricature.

Ken Gill and Clive Jenkins became joint general secretaries of MSF, before Jenkins retired in 1988, when Ken paid tribute to his role in: 'organising the unorganisable.'

On retirement from MSF, he received a golden handshake and he had also been able to make a killing during the property boom. This allowed him to move in style to Tasmania where he bought a yacht he cheekily christened Affluent Society.

As Paul Routledge, perhaps a little uncharitably, put it: 'He departed like the proverbial Cheshire Cat, leaving behind only his trademark sneer.' Sadly, his death in 1999 went virtually unnoticed.

" When Jenkins was on a trade union delegation to the USA he asked why so many trade unionists carry guns, and was told: 'That's how we resolve inter-union disputes here.' Jenkins quipped back: 'It's not dissimilar to what we do in Britain but we call it Bridlington!' "

ALAN JINKINSON steered the merger process between NALGO, NUPE and COHSE in 1993 to create UNISON the biggest public service union in the country. He remained general secretary until 1996, when he retired to be succeeded by Rodney Bickerstaffe.

Jinkinson was a consistent campaigner for better pay and conditions for public sector workers. In the late 1970s, seeking to ban local authorities from discriminating on the grounds of sexual orientation, he was met with cries of 'no, no, never, never,' from Tory councillors.

He was certainly of the left and in 1983 Jinkinson and Ron Todd were 'volunteered' by their respective General Secretaries to organise the 'People's March for Jobs'.

A strong supporter of a minimum wage he clashed vigorously with Blair over the party's decision to abandon a target figure.

He proudly oversaw Britain's first television advertising campaign by a union – the award-winning 'Slow-witted, but powerful bear versus the collective power of small ants'

It was a big hit and underlined the 'old Labour' message of how collective strength can bring success.

Instead of adopting the 'modernist' approach of marketing services to members', the union went for a humorous yet unmistakable message that collective action is all-important. Jinkinson said: 'The message is simple – it's the basis of trade unionism – strength in numbers for the collective good.'

Always a non-conformist, in l987 Jinkinson refused for a number of hours to accept service of a High Court Order banning NALGO from campaigning politically after a General Election had been called – not believing that the person claiming to 'execute' the Order could possibly be called Pierrepoint. Embarrassingly, that was indeed the poor man's name.

JACK JONES was christened James Larkin Jones, after the renowned Irish union leader James Larkin. This was very prescient because he became the epitome of a great trade union leader.

He was elected general secretary of the Transport and General Workers' Union (TGWU) in 1968 and led the union for nine years. During that time he held many prominent positions in the TUC and was a principal spokesman on international and economic matters.

Born in Liverpool, he left school at 14 and worked as an engineering apprentice, then as a dock-worker. He served with the British Battalion of the XV International Brigade in the Spanish Civil War and was seriously wounded at the Battle of Ebro in 1938. On his return to England he became a full-time official of the T&G in Coventry.

As Regional Secretary of the union, Jones played a key role in organising the workforce of the West Midlands motor industry in the post-war period and was instrumental in building up what became the first national and hugely influential shop stewards' movement.

He was a true internationalist and went to Chile on a trade union delegation, after Pinochet's coup, to try and free imprisoned trade unionists. He was thrown out by the junta, but before being bundled on to the plane, he shouted out: 'This is what fascists do to a visitor from a friendly country!' for all to hear.

After retirement he threw himself into campaigning for better treatment of Britain's pensioners. He also remained true to his working class principles and refused the offer of a peerage.

'Win or lose,' he used to say, 'the world needs sincerity'. And that he certainly had in abundance.

In the final paragraph of his biography Jack writes:

> Despite its opponents and critics, trade unionism is needed more than ever today to secure equality and justice at work and in society. It is needed to grapple with the problems of technological change and multi-national companies. My hope is that it will grow in the spirit of internationalism, helping the poor of the world to rise from their poverty and strengthening the efforts for world peace. Is it a dream? I do not think so.

The sign held reads: FROM SPANISH CIVIL WAR TO DECENT BRITISH PENSIONS

KEITH JOSEPH (1918-1994), later Baron Joseph of Portsoken, was a barrister and Conservative cabinet minister under three different prime ministers. He was widely regarded as the power behind the throne and the leading theoretician of what came to be known as Thatcherism – the application of the strictest monetarist economics to Britain in the seventies and eighties.

Joseph's rambling speeches, packed with equally rambling political philosophy, led to him being caricatured as The Mad Monk, in reference to his dour, puritanical appearance and pontificating style.

He inadvertently shot himself in the political foot with his infamous 'eugenics' speech attacking single mothers, which caused widespread outrage, forcing him to step down in favour of Margaret Thatcher in the contest for the leadership of the Conservative Party: 'Yet these mothers, the under-twenties in many cases, single parents, from classes 4 and 5, are now producing a third of all births. A high proportion of these births are a tragedy for the mother, the child and for society. Yet proposals to extend birth-control facilities to these classes of people, particularly young unmarried girls, the potentially young unmarried mothers, evokes entirely understandable moral opposition. Is it not condoning immorality? I suppose it is.'

According to Michael Fitzgerald, Professor of Child and Adolescent Psychiatry at Trinity College Dublin:

    Joseph had Asperger's syndrome, an autistic condition that renders sufferers unable to interpret social situations or to empathise with other people.

NEIL KINNOCK (born 1942), later Baron Kinnock of Bedwellty. An only child, he was born in Tredegar, South Wales. His father was a coal miner who suffered from dermatitis and had to find work as a labourer; his mother was a district nurse.

Kinnock went to university, obtaining a degree (at the second attempt) in industrial relations and history. A year later, Kinnock obtained a postgraduate diploma in education and he later worked as a tutor for the Workers' Educational Association (WEA).

Another Welshman with the proverbial gift of the gab, he was admired in his early years as an MP for his fiery, passionate speeches on behalf of working people and for justice. Like so many who set out on the left of the Labour Party, he slowly drifted rightward as his career progressed.

The biggest disappointment was his letting the miners down during the big strike of 1984. Despite a number of appeals for him, as leader of the Labour Party, to speak at miners' meetings, he always found an excuse not to.

He was a Member of Parliament from 1970 to 1995, and Leader of the Opposition and Labour Party leader from 1983 to 1992, when he resigned after the 1992 general election defeat.

He was rewarded by Tony Blair and eased into a lucrative job as a UK Commissioner in the EU from 1995 until 2004, before being given a peerage, and is now Chairman of the British Council and President of Cardiff University.

Ken recalls:

66 **When I'd been expelled from the Communist Party after the Democratic Left faction took it over, Kinnock was asked by a journalist if I'd now be admitted to the Labour Party. He replied diplomatically; 'As far as I am aware he hasn't applied to join yet.'** 99

ROGER LYONS became General Secretary of MSF from 1992. He later became Joint General Secretary of Amicus, when the union merged with the Amalgamated Union of Engineers and Electricians in 2002.

Lyons was a long-standing member of the Trade Union Friends of Israel.

After over 30 years, his career ended with many accusations about the purging of left-wingers from the union and much publicised concern over his expenses claims, as well as his attempts to cling on to office.

In 2004 he was removed from his post, following a ruling of the Trades Union Certification Officer.

Justifying buying a radio for his bathroom on union expenses, Lyons told a journalist: 'My wife hates hearing the Today programme when we are in bed. I could listen to our own radio with earphones, but it is not very satisfactory so I go into the bathroom to hear the programme on the union's radio.'

❝ In Amicus, Lyons' extraordinary expense account lifestyle earned him the nick-name of 'Roger the Dodger'. ❞

MICK MCGAHEY (1925–1999) was a Scottish miners' leader and life-long Communist who described himself as 'a product of my class and my movement.' His miner father, John, was a founder member of the Communist Party of Great Britain and took an active part in the General Strike of 1926.

Mick started work aged 14 at the Gateside Colliery, and continued to work as a miner for the next 25 years. He followed his father into the Communist Party and was a lifelong member of the National Union of Mineworkers (NUM). He remained a member of the Communist Party until its dissolution in 1990. Mick was also an implacable defender of the Soviet Union, seeing the latter as a beacon of hope for humanity.

He was elected national Vice-President of the NUM in 1972 and when addressing union conferences he would invariably stress that the Labour Movement was just that – a movement not a monument; a living organisation, not a fossil. And in hard-fought debates with those who opposed what he saw as sensible policies, he would suggest that they were intent on 'adopting a monopoly on stupidity.'

McGahey was a fiery and passionate orator and his distinctive, gravelly voice was immediately recognisable in any company. He combined a steely public charisma with an auld Scots gentlemanly manner in private, which made him even more dangerous in the eyes of the establishment.

He was widely recognised as a wise and pragmatic negotiator and he played a key role in the 1984/5 miners' strike which he supported to the end, even though he had his qualms about some of the tactics.

And, as Ken depicts him, he was always dressed in tie and suit.

66 'To represent the working class', McGahey would say, 'one should be dressed in one's best'. 99

ADA MADDOCKS OBE (1927-2007) was an early woman president of the TUC and one of the few prominent women trade unionists of her day. .

She was a national health officer for NALGO (the National Association of Local Government Officers), which is now part of UNISON. She served on the TUC general council from 1977 until 1991 and in 1990 became only the fifth woman to hold the office of president.

During the bitter ambulance workers' dispute of 1989-90 Ada, TUC president at the time, gave unstinting support to all involved. She even went to London's Smithfield market one cold winter's morning, well before dawn, to win the meat porters' support for the ambulance workers. They even let her speak from one of their barrows – an honour previously only enjoyed by the Queen Mother.

Her time on the TUC coincided both with a growth in the prominence of women in the trade union movement and the unions' battle against their most formidable woman opponent, Margaret Thatcher.

When she joined the TUC she was one of just two women (the other being Marie Patterson, of the T&G) elected to the seats traditionally reserved for women to ensure that the council was not entirely an all-male club.

By the time she left, she was one of 15 women on the 50-member body, and the slogan that 'a woman's place was in her union' was one with which few trade unionists would disagree.

In retirement, Ada remained active in her local community and was a keen supporter of Age Concern.

66 Ada was always the scorer at the annual pre-Congress cricket match between the General Council and the Hacks. When she retired, Alan Jinkinson (former General Secretary of Nalgo, then UNISON) was handed the onerous task. That year the Hacks won by the extremely narrow margin of three runs. At the traditional drinks ceremony given afterwards by the TUC General Secretary for the players, John Monks upbraided Alan saying: 'Ada would never have allowed such a thing to happen'. 99

NELSON MANDELA was the first President of South Africa chosen in a fully representative democratic election. Before his presidency (1994–1999), Mandela was an anti-apartheid activist and leader of the African National Congress's armed wing Umkhonto we Sizwe.

The South African courts convicted him on charges of terrorism in the infamous Treason Trials and he served 27 years in prison, spending most of them on the unforgivingly harsh Robben Island.

Ken met him on several occasions but never had the time to draw him until he happened to be in Dublin when Mandela spoke to the Irish Anti-Apartheid Movement where this quick sketch was made.

Mandela's opposition to apartheid made him a symbol of freedom and equality. Following his release from prison on 11 February 1990, he promoted reconciliation and negotiation, helping lead the transition towards multi-racial democracy in South Africa.

He has become a symbol throughout the world, across the political spectrum, for his principled positions, political integrity, deep humanity and supreme dignity.

Mandela has received more than one hundred awards over four decades, most notably the Nobel Peace Prize in 1993. He is currently the world's most celebrated elder statesman who continues to voice his opinion on topical issues.

In South Africa he is often known as Madiba, an honorary title given to elders of his clan and often alluded to by the international media.

He once tellingly and memorably said:

> Through its imperialist system Britain brought about untold suffering to millions of people. And this is a historical fact. To be able to admit this would increase the respect we have for British institutions.

ROBERT MAXWELL (1923-1991), aka 'Cap'n Bob', was a member of ASTMS and always referred to Ken as 'Mr General Secretary' or 'My General Secretary'.

Ken recalls that he had fingers in lots of pies and that they often met at east European embassy receptions.

'It had been reported that Maxwell had ordered German presses for his Daily Mirror print shop rather than British-made ones,' Ken recalls. 'So I, in an editorial of the union's journal, accused him of being a hypocrite: that he carried the British flag on the masthead of his paper The Daily Mirror but didn't support British manufacturing.

'He rang me and told me he was sueing me for £1 million for defamation. It turned out the report was inaccurate – Maxwell had tried to buy British but the company couldn't deliver, so he was forced to go abroad. Once I heard the true story I apologised and the matter was laid to rest with a handshake. Maxwell said 'I won't forget your support.'

But he could be a brute. When I visited his office at The Mirror on one occasion, he ordered a journalist on the paper, who later became a British ambassador, to go and get coffees and smoked salmon sandwiches for us; he treated everyone like errand boys.

With the plundering of his own employees' pension fund to fund his reckless speculation, he came to symbolise par excellence the unacceptable face of capitalism.

Ken's recollection of Maxwell is that:

" He was probably my most cantankerous member. On one occasion a group of members were calling for his expulsion from the union because of his tactics as an employer, but I knew if we tried to expel him he would take us to court. He loved threatening to sue one and all for millions. I was always walking on a tightrope between him and my justifiably irate members. "

BILL MORRIS became the first black leader of a British trade union. This was a great achievement, bearing in mind he had arrived as a sixteen year-old immigrant from a poor family in the West Indies. He was General Secretary of the T&GWU from 1991 to 2003, but to many he was rather a disappointment.

He made the pertinent point during his election campaign:

66 **I am not the black candidate, rather the candidate who is black.** 99

He was particularly criticised for his leadership over the lock out of Liverpool dockers by the Mersey Docks and Harbour Company in 1996, which ended in defeat.

He became very close to the New Labour leadership and received a knighthood in the 2003 Queen's birthday honours list. In April 2006 he became a life peer and took his seat in the House of Lords.

LEN MURRAY (1922 – 2004), later Baron Murray of Epping Forest. He was born in Hadley, Shropshire, the son of a farm worker. He became a teacher for a short time and a Methodist lay preacher.

He served in the army during the Second World War, but was sent home with combat exhaustion from Normandy after D-Day, when he had the opportunity during his convalescence to read voraciously and to study left-wing literature.

His left-wing sentiments were later reinforced by his taking a job as a storeman in a Wolverhampton factory and he sold the Daily Worker on street corners. Len also joined the Communist Party for a short time.

Later he went to New College, Oxford, where he gained a First in Philosophy, Politics and Economics.

He was General Secretary of the TUC from 1973–1984, and played a key role during the 'Winter of Discontent' in 1978/79, and in confrontations with Margaret Thatcher's government.

Ron Todd said of Murray: 'He had the respect of both left and right and he did not mince his words. He was straight as a die. He also had the knack of sitting with a problem and deploying a logic with which one could not disagree.'

In 1979 after the election of Margaret Thatcher, Murray said:

❝ I was simply astonished that Thatcher declined to change direction despite industrial conflict and ever more appalling economic conditions. ❞

TERRY PARRY was General Secretary of the Fire Brigades Union (FBU) from 1964 until 1980 during a difficult and turbulent period.

The national strike of 1977 followed the government imposition of a 10% pay limit that formed part of a wider settlement that spanned the military and police.

Parry, somewhat reluctantly, defended the government's 'social contract', claiming that the fight against inflation took priority over fire fighters' sectional interests.

This attitude cost him much support among his members.

Ken recounts being asked by Parry to do him a favour:

" Once at the TUC there was a large picket of very angry firemen gathered outside demanding that Terry come down and meet them. He said to me: 'Will you go instead and talk to them? If I go they'll kick me to pieces but you'll be OK'. He was actually suffering from very bad legs, so his fears were justified on health grounds. Being young, and inexperienced I agreed and went down to placate them, but they jostled and barracked me just the same. "

MARIE PATTERSON was the T&G National Women's Officer until 1984, when she retired. She was one of the tiny handful of women since 1868 to become president of the TUC.

Marie was, though, even more rare: because of the illness of a colleague, she became president of Congress twice – a factor that was, on occasions, a mixed blessing.

She was generally regarded as a competent Chair and chairing conferences is an onerous task for anyone. On one occasion when she was in the Chair, an agitated Ricky Tomlinson burst into a conference.

This was when Tomlinson was still a building worker and before he became renowned as an actor and media personality. He ran around the hall to avoid being caught and expelled by the stewards, demanding to be given the opportunity to speak on behalf of the convicted Shrewsbury building workers.

In the pandemonium that ensued Marie was hard pressed to calm conference down. Jack Jones suggested to her that she let Ricky have his say, and order was restored.

On another occasion while chairing the annual Congress, a hand vote was carried which called for the immediate expulsion of the biggest union in the country – her own. After a fraught but short adjournment, delegates returned to reverse the decision in order to avert the consequences of such a disastrous decision.

However, these two amusing anecdotes should not deflect from the undoubted contribution she made to enhancing the profile of women in the trade union movement and to the work of Congress.

When she saw Ken's caricature, her comment was:

" **We women don't like his insulting drawings and he should cease producing anymore forthwith.** "

Ken says: "I found many women were offended by my caricatures, so I stuck largely to drawing men, which was not difficult as there were, at that time, few women in key positions anyway. I gathered, in fact, that Marie was far from pleased with this drawing I did of her."

JOHN PRESCOTT was elected Deputy Leader of the Labour Party in 1994 and appointed Deputy Prime Minister after Labour's victory in the 1997 General Election. Known as 'Prezza' and 'Two Jags' in tabloid speak on account of his personal Jaguar car fleet, Prescott is the son of a railway signalman and grandson of a miner. Born in Prestatyn, north Wales, he became a steward and waiter in the Merchant Navy.

He worked for Cunard and was a popular left-wing union activist. He was also a capable boxer, as one unfortunate heckler found out to his cost during the 2001 general election campaign.

In his trade union days, Prescott had a reputation as a firebrand. He was known as a Red and played an active role in the 1966 seamen's strike. At that time, merchant seamen faced bitter opposition from the Labour government, which imposed a state of emergency and threatened to use the navy and even the RAF to break the strike.

Prime Minister Harold Wilson said the country was being held to ransom by a 'tightly knit group of politically-motivated men', which was taken up as a hue and cry by the tabloid press. Among the leaders, apart from Prescott, were several members of the Communist Party.

Prescott was often pilloried by the press for his massacring of the English language, but this smacked of condescension towards a working class bloke who'd climbed the ladder.

'I supported Prescott's leadership bid in 1994,' says Ken. 'After his defeat he presented me with a putty medal, on which was inscribed: "He who dares loses".'

Blair was happy to have Prescott as Deputy Leader to provide a proletarian fig-leaf for his Thatcherite New Labour policies. He was, it was felt, ideally suited to keep the traditional old Labourites and the trade unions in line.

He has recently been quoted as saying quite refreshingly:

❝ I don't want to be a member of the House of Lords. I will not accept it. My wife Pauline would quite like me to accept it, but why should I be sidelined to the Lords when I could do so much more for the Labour movement? ❞

BERT RAMELSON (born 1910 in the Ukraine died 1994). He was the son of a Jewish rabbi, and could actually remember the Russian revolution taking place. His two older sisters joined the Bolsheviks and remained in the Soviet Union.

Ramelson emigrated to Canada in 1921, with the rest of the family. Then, in 1937, after a year as a barrister, he went to fight in Spain and was a Lieutenant in the `Macpaps` (the McKenzie-Pappineau battlion), the Canadian battalion of the International Brigade.

Settling in Britain in 1939, he worked for a time as a trainee manager at Marks and Spencer. In 1939, he married Marion Jessop, the author of a pioneering work of feminist history, Petticoat Rebellion.

He was a tank commander during the Second World War and was captured by the Germans at Tobruk in 1941. In 1943, after organising an extraordinary mass break out from his prisoner of war camp, he linked up with Italian partisans who organised his return to Britain. He then served in India for a time.

Ramelson became a full time worker for the Communist Party in 1953. He became the Party's National Industrial Organiser, a role that was to confirm him as a man at the very core of British politics. He was a powerful orator and effective pamphleteer. He played a key role in most of the industrial battles that took place in Britain throughout the latter half of the 20th century. He was admired throughout the labour movement for his acumen and principled advice, just as he was respected, but also feared, by the employers and right-wing politicians.

A man of powerful intellect, he was especially noted for his strategic thinking. An aspect of this was the care and attention he paid to the long-term personal development of countless individual trade unionists. He also played a key role in the successes of the left in the trade unions during the 1960s and 1970s, especially in the vital matter of maintaining independence from the state.

Ramelson was accused by Prime Minister Harold Wilson of being the ring-leader of a tight-knit conspiracy to subvert democracy during the seamen's strike of 1966. It still makes Ken collapse with laughter:

“ Anyone who knew Bert would realise this was nonsense. He always spoke so loudly, at the top of his voice, that anyone within a mile could hear every word he said. If you wanted to have a conspiracy Bert was the last person you'd invite to join you! ”

ALAN SAPPER (1931-2006) was general secretary of the Association of Cinematograph, Television and Allied Technicians (ACCT) from 1969 to 1991.

He and his brother Laurie were always men of the left. Laurie had been General Secretary of the Association of University Teachers (AUT) and was a member of the Communist Party; Alan was a fellow traveller. He was an implacable negotiator with the employers and during his leadership the ACTT remained one of the strongest of the craft unions with a strict closed shop which resulted in its members enjoying relatively high wages and top conditions.

Though at opposite ends of the political spectrum, he and Frank Chapple sat next to each other throughout their time on the General Council and as vice president of Congress it fell to Alan to present the TUC gold badge to the electricians' leader at the end of Chapple's presidential year, an act Sapper said at the time felt like Dracula presenting Godzilla with a Blue Peter Badge!

Alan enjoyed fine wine and good food and was a regular at his favourite corner table at the Gay Hussar at lunchtimes from where he could watch the politicians come and go and note who was dining with whom. The restaurant was conveniently situated around the corner from ACTT's headquarters in Soho Square. As in life so in death, Alan insisted that he be buried in a simple cardboard coffin to leave more cash to spend on entertaining his friends at the wake.

He was also a director of Ealing Studios from 1994 to 2000 and chaired the League for Democracy in Greece from 1970 until 2000.

Ken recalled an example of Alan's sharp wit from a meeting organised by Elwyn Jones, Attorney General under Wilson (and the father of the left-wing artist Dan Jones) of legal figures and trade union officials at Windsor Castle, of all places:

66 **A judge attending the meeting arrived late and complained: 'Awfully sorry I'm late, but I was held up. It's all those damned strikers and pickets everywhere; what's this country coming to?' Alan Sapper, one of the trade union officials present retorted: 'I see what you mean; if you people came out on strike no one would notice!** 99

TOM SAWYER later Baron Sawyer, was General Secretary of the Labour Party from 1994 to 1998.

Sawyer worked in engineering before moving into trade unionism where he rose to become Deputy General Secretary of NUPE and served through its merger to become UNISON until 1994.

He became a director of several companies, amongst them, ironically, one supplying agency nurses to the NHS and public sector bodies.

Ken's cartoon refers to the overstaged Labour Party rally in Sheffield, a week ahead of the 1992 general election. The event was held in an indoor sports venue and was attended by 10,000 Labour Party members, including the entire shadow cabinet, and is reported to have cost some £100,000; Kinnock, was flown in by helicopter. It was modelled on American presidential campaign conventions.

At one point in the proceedings, Kinnock and the shadow cabinet paraded onto the stage from the back of the hall, walking through an increasingly enthusiastic audience –

the next government Cabinet in waiting – culminating in an emotional and hyper-active Kinnock taking the podium and shouting 'We're all right! We're all right!', followed by 'We'd better get some talking done here, serious talking'.

Ahead of the event, Labour was polling well ahead of the Conservative Party, but this was dramatically reduced the following day, with Gallup placing the Conservatives ahead of Labour.

66 **The fall in the opinion polls was largely blamed on the rally, which many considered brash, American, triumphalist and self-congratulatory, and Kinnock's performance was viewed as not the way the British do things. It was lampooned by JAK in the Evening Standard as reminiscent of a nazi Nuremburg rally.** 99

In the end the election was a victory for the Conservatives. Although according to Murdoch's favourite tabloid, 'It was 'The Sun wot won it'.

HUGH SCANLON (1913–2004), known affectionately as 'Hughie', was apprenticed at 14 as an instrument maker to a local engineering firm where he first joined his union, the Amalgamated Engineering Union (AEU).

He later became a shop steward, then convenor, before joining the Communist Party in 1937 following the events of the Spanish Civil War. He made use of its networks and organising skills to rise through the union, becoming a district official in 1947.

He left the Party in 1954 but continued as a broad left candidate within the union, winning the leadership in 1968. Scanlon and T&G leader Jack Jones were known by the press as 'The Terrible Twins' for their opposition to both Labour Party and Conservative Party attempts to restrict the power of the unions and control wages.

However, when Labour returned to office in 1974, the two became the prime advocates within the union movement for the acceptance of the proposed Social Contract which would impose wage controls and limits on strike action.

This battle, culminating in the 'Winter of Discontent', led to the defeat of the Labour Party in the 1979 elections. Scanlon's politics led to him being effectively blacklisted between 1966 and 1977 on the recommendation of the British Secret Service.

In 1977, he was prevented from becoming chairman of British Shipbuilders because MI5 advised that he should not see documents marked as confidential or secret.

He memorably said:

66 **Once you've understood the theory of surplus value, you're a socialist for life.** 99

ARTHUR SCARGILL was President of the National Union of Mineworkers (NUM) from 1982 until 2001. He founded and currently leads the Socialist Labour Party.

He first made his name as the militant regional official who, with the help of the local Communist Party, directed the decisive and victorious picketing of the Saltley Gates power station in Birmingham during the 1972 miners' strike. Scargill described it as 'the greatest day in my life'.

On becoming General Secretary in 1981, he was confronted with a government under Margaret Thatcher which was determined to smash the strong mineworkers' union, the most powerful working class organisation that stood in the way of savage neoliberal reforms of the economy to be initiated by comprehensive pit closures.

Prophetically Scargill warned that coal mining in Britain would be finished if the government got its way. The national strike begun in 1984 was one of the most bitter and confrontational of any previous industrial dispute apart from the 1926 General Strike. It lasted until March 1985.

The Thatcher government had prepared well for the strike, with press and police force ready to do all it took to smash it. The strike became a symbolic struggle but ended with the defeat of the NUM by the Conservative government.

The door was prised open for its free market programme.

The dispute exposed deep divisions in British society and caused considerable bitterness, especially in northern England, Scotland and in south Wales where mining communities were destroyed.

Ken is unequivocal that: 'whatever one's views on Scargill, few would challenge his commitment to miners' families everywhere and to the mining industry. His declaration that Thatcher would decimate the industry if she weren't challenged was pooh-poohed at the time, but the reality became worse than even he foresaw.'

On a lighter note Ken tells the following anecdote:

66 I was in South Africa as a member of a delegation, together with Arthur Scargill, to attend the retirement party for Cyril Ramaphosa*. Mandela who was there told Scargill that he had looked up to him as his working class hero when he was on Robben Island. I thought I wouldn't get Arthur back down on the ground after that! 99

* Ramaphosa was the first General Secretary of the National Union of Mineworkers, a position he held until he resigned in June 1991, following his election as Secretary General of the African National Congress (ANC).

MIKE SEIFERT has been a progressive solicitor for over 40 years and a communist since 1960. He has represented a number of unions with left wing leaderships including the National Union of Mineworkers throughout their historic strike during the eighties and the unions led by Ken Gill.

He has been the (unpaid) lawyer for the Morning Star for more than 30 years and has also represented overseas clients including Cuba, the Anti-Apartheid Movement, the ANC and the National Liberation Front of South Vietnam as well as the Socialist Republic of Vietnam.

He was one of the leading organisers of the movement to free Angela Davis when she was being hounded in the US by the FBI in the seventies.

He is still practising law and is currently engaged in a series of legal matters on behalf of Greenpeace.

Mike has a gently edifying story relating to this caricature:

66 Ken was very pleased when I used this drawing in my election leaflet when standing for a seat on the local council. It is not a particularly flattering portrait – unshaven, with a fag in my hand – but it brought me some goodwill and a number of people said they voted communist for the first time because of the 'honesty and humour' of the drawing. 99

DEREK SIMPSON was the first and only general secretary of Amicus the trade union. When the T&G merged with Amicus in 2007 he became joint General Secretary with Tony Woodley of Unite. Both men had risen from the shop floor and have strong left-wing views.

Simpson has suggested that:

> by picking a fight with the unions and siding with the bosses, Labour is in danger of betraying its industrial soul.

He issued a 'call to arms for activists to seize back the party from middle-class pseudo-liberal thinkers who exploit apathy and discourage working people from participating so that the field is then left clear for their supposedly intellectually superior middle-ground attitudes.'

Derek Simpson's affection for his mobile in the caricature is but a recognition of what a magnificent tool it has become for the committed union organiser. Twenty five years ago the miners' attacked from all sides by the repressive forces of the state, could have achieved marvels with these at their disposal. Rather than having to dash every time to a phone booth down the road only to find it vandalised or otherwise out of commission, instant on the spot communications might have significantly altered the course of that legendary, heroic strike.

BILL SIRS was General Secretary of the Iron and Steel Trades Confederation (ISTCU) which later became the Community union after merger with the National Union of Knitwear, Footwear and Apparel Trades (KFAT) in 2004.

Community began advocating 'Community Unionism' which was to promote the improvement of conditions in the workplace as well as in the general community in which its members lived.

Sirs was always regarded as a stalwart of the 'moderate' wing of the trade union movement, always cautious and never taking a militant position even during the Thatcher period which saw the once mighty British steel industry slowly run down.

His union also prevaricated about helping the miners during the national strike in the eighties, at a cricial time, when a joint approach could have helped save both industries.

Ken recalls him as:

A keen proselytiser for healthier living. When most of his fellow union leaders thought exercise meant a short walk to the bar, he would be out doing mini-marathons. His prescient efforts to ban smoking at TUC events caused a predictable outcry by the then powerful Tobacco Workers Union.

JOHN SMITH (1938–1994) served as leader of the Labour Party from July 1992 until his sudden and unexpected death from a heart attack.

Smith was elected as MP for North Lanarkshire in 1970 and when James Callaghan became Prime Minister, Smith became a Minister of State at the Privy Council Office.

He piloted the highly controversial devolution proposals for Scotland and Wales through the House of Commons and was later appointed Secretary of State for Trade.

Neil Kinnock chose him as his Shadow Chancellor in 1987 after the Labour Party's General Election defeat.

Despite a quiet, modest manner and his politically moderate stance, Smith was a witty and often scathing speaker and was named Parliamentarian of the Year twice.

As Labour leader he presided over the abolition of the trade union block vote at Labour party conferences, and replaced it with 'one member one vote' at the 1993 conference. He also committed a future Labour government to establishing a Scottish Parliament.

In a debate in the House of Commons in 1993, Smith wittily exposed the Conservative Government's inadequacies by referring to their defeat in the Newbury by-election, and a subsequent Cabinet reshuffle thus:

66 **If we were to offer that tale of events to the BBC Light Entertainment Department as a script, I think that the producers of 'Yes, Minister' would have turned it down as hopelessly over the top.** 99

When John Smith died unexpectedly, one of the more arcane conspiracy theories doing the rounds had the Fabians eliminating Smith as he was seen as an obstacle to their dastardly plans to take over the Labour Party and make it a clone of the Tories. The incontrovertible proof is 'dead' simple: Blair and Brown are Fabians but Smith wasn't, also their surnames start with a B and his didn't – hard evidence difficult to ignore.

NORMAN TEBBIT, later Baron Tebbit, was one of the Tory Party's most notorious MPs. Born into a working class family, he was elected MP for Epping in 1970 and then for Chingford in 1974. He was a member of the right-wing Conservative Monday Club and was invariably characterised as an Essex 'boot boy' in reference to his constituency, and his bullying tactics.

During the Grunwick dispute, when the overwhelmingly female Asian workforce struck over pay and working conditions, owner George Ward refused to recognise their union. There was a split in the Conservative Shadow Cabinet between the moderates, lead by Jim Prior and the hawks, lead by Keith Joseph and Norman Tebbit as to what action, if any, to take.

Michael Foot described Tebbit tellingly during a 1978 parliamentary debate when he referred to him as a 'semi-house-trained polecat'.

As Thatcher's Employment Secretary, he introduced the notorious Employment Act of 1982, which he believed was his 'greatest achievement in Government'.

'The Tebbit era ushered in a new confrontational and aggressive attitude towards trade unions', Ken says. 'Until then even Conservative ministers had maintained a civility in relations, but Tebbit made no bones about how he hated the unions and always said: "I've no time to talk to you."'

In the aftermath of the1981 urban riots, Tebbit responded to a suggestion that rioting was the natural reaction to unemployment: 'I grew up in the thirties with an unemployed father,' he declared. 'He didn't riot. He got on his bike and looked for work, and he kept looking until he found it.'

This exchange was the origin of the attribution to Tebbit of the slogan "On yer bike!" which inspired this caricature. However, Ken points out that:

66 **In his autobiography, Upwardly Mobile, Tebbit reproduced my cartoon of him on his bike, crediting it but he never asked my permission to use it.** 99

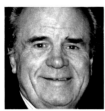

RON TODD (1927-2005) was general secretary of the Transport and General Workers Union from 1985 to 1992. An east Londoner, he served in the Royal Marines in Hong Kong during the Second World War, an experience which brought home to him the extent of inequality in the world. 'I became convinced that the only route to people's improvement was through collective action,' he said.

Ron was known throughout the trade union movement for his passionate commitment to peace and international solidarity. He kept the T&GWU in the forefront of campaigns for nuclear disarmament and against apartheid in South Africa.

Following his retirement, Ron continued to live in east London. He retained a close association with the T&G and also contributed poetry on a regular basis to the union's publications.

❝ When Eric Hammond General Secretary of the EETPU during a debate at the TUC about the miners strike said that they 'were lions led by donkeys' Ron's riposte was as instantaneous as it was razor sharp: 'I'd rather be a donkey than a jackal.' ❞

When Ron became seriously ill with leukemia, and realised he hadn't long to live, he rang Rodney Bickerstaffe and told him he would like him to read the eulogy at his funeral. Rodney, perhaps not realising how serious Ron's condition was, replied: 'Let me get my diary; what date were you thinking of?'

LECH WALESA (born 1943) was a shipyard electrician in Gdynia and a co-founder of Solidarnosc, Poland's first independent trade union. He won the Nobel Peace Prize in 1983 and served as President of Poland from 1990 to 1995.

Walesa acted as an informal leader of the opposition during the talks in 1990 which culminated in the Polish United Workers Party relinquishing state power and agreeing to hold open and contested elections to the Polish parliament.

He was the first non-head of state to address a joint meeting of the US Congress in November 1989 and the first recipient of the US Presidential Medal of Liberty in the same year.

As president of Poland, he promised the earth – or rather that Poland would be transformed into a second Japan.

Once out of the limelight, Walesa withdrew from political life to head a nebulous institute named after himself. He is said to lack even an elementary sense of humour and of being extraordinarily touchy.

Not unlike George 'Dubya' Bush, he was prone to uttering nonsensical phrases, such as: 'I'm definitely for it and even against it' or 'There are pluses which are positive and pluses that are negative.'

Walesa is a devout, if ostentatious Roman Catholic, who has repeatedly said that his faith always helped him during Solidarity's difficult moments. Once a woman approached him at an official meeting asking that he listen to her as she was 'sent by God' to which he replied, in all seriousness: 'That's great, me too.'

Ken recalls:

> At a TUC dinner given in Walesa's honour in 1989, before the demise of the socialist government in Warsaw, he unexpectedly told us, in private and rather embarrassingly, that Britain should take advantage of the abundance of cheap Polish labour once the Communists had been overthrown. How prophetic!

NORMAN WILLIS became Assistant General Secretary of the TUC in 1974 and General Secretary from 1984-93. He was President of the European Trade Union Confederation (ETUC) from 1991–93.

The leadership of Willis at the TUC coincided in the late 1980s with a period of concerted attacks on the trade union movement by Conservative governments.

Union membership was falling and the Labour Party was conducting a fundamental review of its policies and the nature of its links with the unions. He was perhaps not the greatest general secretary the TUC has ever had, but he certainly wasn't the worst and he held office during a particularly difficult period.

Ken says: 'It was unfortunate that the big miners' strike took place during his stint at Congress House. On one occasion, at its height, Willis was obliged to address a meeting of angry miners with a hangman's noose held dangling above his head. Willis didn't manage to bring this bitter strike to an honourable conclusion, but with the Thatcher government on a warpath it was probably a dauntless task.

He also had two endearing hobbies: embroidery and versifying. Guardian journalist Ian Aitkin recalled that his party piece at many a trade union gathering was performing one of his parodies of well known songs, one of which was:

66 **I am the man, the very fat man, what waters the workers' beer.** 99

MICHAEL HESELTINE, nicknamed Tarzan after a Steve Bell cartoon, later became Baron Heseltine. He resigned as Secretary of State for Defence over the Westland Affair, when he supported British helicopter manufacturing against Thatcher's preference for US supplier Sikorsky. A gifted PR man, he took on the Campaign for Nuclear Disarmament in the 1983 General Election and oversaw covert surveillance of its offices. Heseltine was a dyed-in-the-wool opponent of the trade unions and the left in general and co-authored many regressive policies.

MARGARET 'MAGGIE' THATCHER, later Baroness Thatcher, was Prime Minister from 1979 until 1990. Leader of the Conservative Party from 1975 to 1990, she is the only woman to hold either post. Thatcher was one of the most right-wing Conservative prime ministers in decades and instigated a massive confrontation with the trade union movement to facilitate the introduction of neo-liberal economics. She called the unions the 'enemy within' and oversaw the introduction of some of the most restrictive union legislation in the western world. Once asked what was her most important political legacy she famously replied:

 Tony Blair and New Labour!

WILLIAM WHITELAW (1918-1999), later 1st Viscount Whitelaw, known affectionately as 'Willie'. Thatcher relied on Whitelaw heavily during his tenure as Deputy Prime Minister and Leader of the Lords, famously announcing that 'every Prime Minister needs a Willie.'

JAMES PRIOR was Secretary of State for Employment from 1979 to 1981. He disagreed with Thatcher on a number of economic issues as well as on the need for draconian anti-union legislation and was seen as one of the cabinet wets.

ANTHONY 'TONY' BLAIR, Prime Minister 1997-2007, pushed through the transformation of the Labour Party into New Labour, ditching socialist policies and distancing it from its founders, the trade unions. He became the Labour Party's longest-serving Prime Minister and the only leader to have taken the party to three consecutive general election victories but dismally low approval ratings forced him to stand down in 2007. When Ken tried to suggest to Blair at a meeting that the policies he was pursuing had been tried before and failed, Blair replied that he was not interested in the past but only in the future! Perhaps he should have added, 'I'm not interested in real issues, but only in my own career.' He will be remembered as the Labour leader who abolished Clause Four and turned Labour into a clone of the Tory Party.

Here is Ken's humorous take on the classic 'leaders of the proletariat' tableau

PAUL ROUTLEDGE, former Labour correspondent of the Daily Mirror has collected over the years many anecdotes some of which have been reproduced in this volume with his kind permission. His The Bumper Book of British Lefties (Politico's 2003) is an ideal biographical source for assorted left-wingers and other rogues.

Frank Chapple taking the
necessary precautions

THE GALLERY It has not been possible to include everyone Ken drew in the main body of this book – that would have made it an over-heavy tome. Those portrayed have been selected largely on the basis of the quality of the drawings, not for their prominence, fame or infamy.

We have addressed this omission by including a selection of drawings without biographical details or anecdotes.

We trust those included here will not feel they have been sidelined to a back-room 'rogues gallery' – no slight is intended, apart from that of the unadorned truth that flowed from the ink of the artist's pen!

Author Salman Rushdie

Lord (Walter) Citrine
TUC General Secretary
(1925-1946) and author of
the 'Bible' of committee
chairmanship: A.B.C. of
Chairmanship: All about
meetings and conferences

Geoffrey Howe Thatcher's
longest-serving Cabinet
minister, successively
holding posts of Chancellor
of the Exchequer, Foreign
Secretary, and finally
Leader of the House of
Commons and Deputy
Prime Minister.

Roy Grantham (APEX General Secretary 1971-1989)

Baron (Garfield) Davies
(General Secretary
USDAW 1986-1997)

David Basnett
(General Secretary
GMB 1973-1985)

Baron Merlyn Rees
(Secretary of State for
Northern Ireland from
1974-1976, then Home
Secretary under
Callaghan)

Jimmy Knapp
(General Secretary
RMT 1983-1990)

Lawrence Daly
(General Secretary
NUM 1968-1984)

A NEW
VIEW
FROM
THE SITE

Peter Lenehan
UCATT Executive
Committee

Bill Keys
General Secretary
of Sogat (1975-1985)

CAN I INTEREST YOU IN A QUIET PRICE FREEZE?

Roy Hattersley
(Deputy Leader of the Labour Party
under Neil Kinnock 1983-1992)

John Lyons
General Secretary of the
Electrical Power Engineers
Association

Pat Turner
GMB National
Women's Officer

Alan Tuffin
General Secretary of Union of
Post Office Workers (UPW)

Sir Gavin Laird
(General Secretary
AEEU 1992-1994)

Mike Walsh
Secretary of the International
Committee of the TUC

Doug Grieve
General Secretary of the
Tobacco Workers Union

Alec Smith
General Secretary
National Union of
Tailors and Garment
Workers NUTGW

Baron (Elwyn) Jones
(Lord Chancellor under
Harold Wilson 1974–1979)

Left Muriel Turner
Deputy General
Secretary of ASTMS

Right Professor
Vic Allen –
official historian
of the NUM

Right Les Dixon
Executive Member
of the AUEW